This Quiet Sun

This Quiet Sun

poems by

Sarah Bein

Red Hen Press

1996

This Quiet Sun

Red Hen Press is a division of Valentine Publishing Group

Cover photograph by Mark E. Cull
Author photograph by Marshall Bein

Edited by Kate Gale

Designed by Mark E. Cull

First Edition
ISBN 1-888996-02-1
Library of Congress Catalog Card Number 96-71326

Red Hen Press
Valentine Publishing Group
P.O. Box 902582
Palmdale, CA 93590-2582

For Heather, Kate and my mother

For a month the almond trees bloomed,
their droppings the delicate silks
we removed when each time a touch
took us closer to the windows where
we whispered *yes*, there on the intricate
balconies of breath, overlooking
the rest of our lives.

— Carolyn Forche
"Poem for Maya"

Contents

This Quiet Sun

Everywhere This Little Boat

It is easy to write in the dark
the light closing in
attaching like I want you to
but you and I travel
in separate boats
you think you will write slowly
I will fall asleep
and when you finish
you will not have this confusion

you will see me
in my rightful place in your universe
a temporary college girlfriend
with violet hair and long fingers
before the woman
the one with a reflection
of pressed on smiles
you see me here in a simple bed
wrapped in sheets

drinking you with a little straw
you are inside me forever
everywhere this little boat
looks for a new direction
for you to fall in water
run your fingers wildly through dirt

you write unstoppable
covered in the water's soil
I am above your bed untamed
you look carefully
sure no one can see you
you are not where you seem to be

A Doctor's Soft Market

she says
we won't be making contributions
for six months

she has watched six months become years
painting floors, renting a house
in this soft market. yes, she says

her pride hiding
six dollar shoes, cloth suits
she looks at her husband

balancing seven checkbooks
crawling to his feet, dishing the words
I love you, like free money

her husband, doctoring Hollywood, upper class
Republican, owns three homes, only renting one
they teach the children to say, We're poor

in this market
her husband is reaching for the neighbors
he feels the synapse, he leaps across it

Tablecloth Dreams

people ask me how I am
I say fine, my parents echo my words
in our family, "fine" is put on tables
eaten ravenously at dinner
we are becoming bulimic

over lunch they ask
if we are feeling well
we answer like monkeys
our food is in our hands

the breath of our formalities
rubs off on everything we touch
our parents are outraged

the tablecloth drapes
puddle on kitchen windows as food
we spin through lies
anyone can see in

Return to Your House, 1968

This is that moment
you had to yourself,
your footsteps follow small animals
collected against your door
small yellow light through the window.

Bits of hair blow on the ground,
you remember a girl who sat with you.
You ran your fingers through
moist new sand. She left quietly,
afraid of what would happen.

For days you had nothing,
your legs underneath you
sitting in a chair in a room
your face showed moons of age
like circles around you dizzying.

This is what you did to yourself.
This is waiting.
You thumb through air,
feel breath leave you
deflate like a rubber raft.

You kept quiet for years,
your mother far away
yet inches from your face.
The breeze outside angers you
bringing with it some small blur of return.

Your body tells you it is not
your childhood you have returned to.
It is something on the edge of your life,
in this room an empty chair a swing
a boy outside waiting

voiceless
his mouth moving
in a language
you no longer
remember.

Gift for My Mother

The sky right before sunrise
is brilliant blue
skin of my skin
you have traveled
the lengths and breadths
of your soul
to open your hands
small and delicate
like the curve of your back
to offer me
blood shoes a space of my own
you are this baby
who is woman strength
tracing the price of lips
you have concluded
that you, mother bearer
have given me yourself
have sent me out
a sculpture a vixen
strong tight knit
like the eyes of a she-wolf
or the feet of a ballerina

The Airplane of Your Mind

I watch you that look in your eye
when your mother walks in the room
your smile dips with your wine glass
ah you say I must be going
the country club Republicans
find your lies with your makeup
melted pools on the floor

when your mother gripped
that 12 inch rope
I suppose
you hopped on the
airplane of your mind
went skiing in the French Alps
shared condos with pretend friends

sitting on the sofa
in the living room
you say you will be flying
first class your next trip over
and I smile
wanting you not to see
that I know

Sharing Fruit

Her eyes smile
she knows lies
she keeps talking

of boys, friends
shopping
anything believable

I suppose her mother
showed her how to reveal
nothing about herself

she waits
gathers other people's lies
like children around her

"What are you afraid of?" she asks
hoping I'll say everything
"Nothing" and her face falls

In my mind
not being beautiful enough
being left alone

Again she says tell me
and waits
hoping I will open

I smile the pasted smile
that has her believing
she does not upset me

she passes strawberries
I pass secrets
Eat it tell me more

The fruit sits in front of us
untouched like her words saying
hug me tell me I'm your best friend

I look at the fruit
touching the outside rim of the plate
Is this normal conversation?

After silence
I am hungry
"I don't feel well" she says

I search what does she want me to say?
I'm sorry you poor thing
Sympathy pity smile

The fruit is arranged neatly
She has everything planned exactly
what I will say what she will say

"I feel hot do I feel hot to you?" she says
"Feel me touch my forehead
Come here be with me share my fruit"

To Heather

she waits for mother
to leave the room
leans and whispers
what she cannot speak

in a pink nightgown
waiting to be her mother
wanting to be wanted

she moves her hands
speaks over the roar
of her childhood

screams to them
curses herself
leaves the room
locks the door

The Yellow Book

In her yellow book
Kashuan shares secrets
with a girl named Vivian
clasped between hands
she writes
of the Japanese Korean War
their hands join in the wind
passing through hallways
they smile
Kashuan walks streets
clasps her book
as white girls scream
she opens the book
she is inside
she closes it
a nervous gesture
outside the book
she cannot see herself
anywhere

Selecting Fruit

Yes
he says
I loved her
I do not know why

we sit together
you tell me this
so I don't think
you are small

all I have told you
you believe
I select pieces of myself
to give to you

I don't know
what you want
what you will do
when silence returns

I think of my words
as gifts
promises
I wrap them carefully

the distance between us is safe
he looks at my clothes hair
looks me over
hands in his lap

checks me like fruit
at the supermarket
eyeing the size
shape color

I think
if you want this
I need to know
I am silent

we take turns
covering ourselves
with words
until we cannot see

each other's eyes
bodies
a replacement
for some dream

Matthew

with the slip of your tongue
you take it away
dreams pinned all summer
on bare white walls
your mother's words hanging
painted over in red
your breath face turns inside out

smog filled construction buildings
fall into piles of dirt
wooden floors small squares linked
bleeding redwood
your broken ankle
European boys carry you five miles
broken cardboard home where you pretended to sleep

while I called you
you made a living of silence
it was all you had
your mother father brothers
stolen hopes lying squashed
between book covers
you always believed you would escape

it was enough at five
your arms already heavy
ceramic post of dirt
watching your life pirouette south
come crashing into my northern life
your voice hung on telephone wires
your life slipped through a current

you say I hold your dreams
we are silent for hours

Where I Left You

you watch me
your eyes on my laugh
what I am wearing
if I think
about you

all you know
is that you are not
supposed to feel this
but you wonder what my hair
would feel like in your hands

conversation circles you
you keep me in your eyes
you have my laugh now
you look outside to trees
moving like legs across this floor

I remember that look
you wanted me to
think of you dream
without you touching me
the fear you could never let go

I am outside as
I think of you
through the window
you stand by yourself
where I left you wondering

I move under this clothing
walk away laughing
pieces of me
fly into your hands
where they crumple

In the Dark

Your hips move
I can't wait any more
I want to touch you
without having you break

Your father surrounds you
you cannot save yourself
I remember the fear
I see in your shaking hands

I remember my mother
looking in my face
uncovering my eyes
for traces of loss

I am outside your window
always outside girl
My hands grip my clothing
I howl Your father is angry

I hear you whispering Speak
so I can hear you Come to me
It is dark in my male world always dark
Dirt covers my shoes

Yours are white your neck bare
I would like to stay
a stone around your neck
a jewel in your ear

Vanishing Into the Bench

You close your eyes,
say she never happened.
I do not smile.
I took you from that vacant hole
in my body and created you beautiful,
but Josh, listen to me. I watch you.
We all watch you vanish into the bench
on which you sit.
My hands are blankets around me.
I write this in losing you.
I licked myself clean.
You are on your knees
looking the other way
you hope nothing
will ever happen to you.
I will be gone
leaving you wrapped in yards
of unwillingness to act, feel.
You do not have eyes.
I was not there to begin with.
Wrap yourself.
Smile at your own face.
Lick your dry lips.
Tell yourself how happy you are.

River Trip

You write me a letter
of boat trips, French rivers
women who would not wait
the French humming "les montagnes"
your boat travels

the longing water
calls your hollow eyes
stifled through currents
the wind carries murmurs
of something like love words

your lips pursed
to the whisper
your mind releases
through this boat
rain echoes everywhere

the pier's wooden poles
cry to you
the Renaissance waits
the wind tears
at pictures

taped by your hammock
letting them fly in the wind

Cardboard Pieces

in the gallery
he stands watching a 5' x 7'
piece of cardboard
The Redheaded Woman in the Garden
talks to him
the man remains
sweat drips
from fluorescent lights
he has made her his own
the man's wife waits for him by the phone
he feels her through everything
the smoke pulsing from his mouth
touches the woman's face
he refuses to believe there is nothing
behind the cardboard
his wife becomes impatient
he feels disloyal
he wishes he could walk away
all that would be left would be him
and the woman
his wife has fallen asleep
the man reaches into his pocket
pulls out another cigarette

Always We End Like This

I came to you in my dreams
slipped my body next to yours
curved your arm around secrets

Three days I stayed with you
inside the rain and cold
we dressed in jeans

Ferried to Long Island through wind
at the cemetery we placed stones
on your grandfather's grave

Afraid to touch you while you talked
of everything, you walked behind me
careful I did not fall

We drive to a lighthouse, the beach
climb stairs to the Atlantic
my hair surrounds us

You stand without speaking
I am cold in the fog
you decide to go back

I cover myself with my arms
I hear you thinking convincing yourself
you want to touch my neck my hands

Three days I feel you all over me
walk miles in the snow
to come to you

I feel your lips on my cheek
whisper goodbye just for a second in your arms
I feel you carefully pull away

We stand on the Eastern most stretch of the country
hold round stones
in our hands

one foot on land one foot in the sea
where each of us
together

walk alone

The Woman's Sunflowers

she sits with Van Gogh sunflowers
on the table, silent
her cracked face
shows disappointment

the petals lie motionless
the center like eyes yellow crying
the woman's hands
block people

flowers collect against her feet
the rain darkens their color
they are less perfect
when darker than hope

underneath flowers and stems
she crosses her legs
uncrosses them
grabs the petals like food

Her Years in Europe

Judy is in the limelight again
the cool rush of December wind
reminds her of European winters
her eyes distant pools of grey
remembering firelight
she hadn't prepared to come back
in her mind she was gone
extinct forever riding horses
through French meadows
living a ghost life
the melody of grass lingers
her life is back there
sleeping in Aix en Provence
the divorce stretched her
across the Atlantic to money
to men reaching to her
a sea of hands
where a sea of grass
used to wave
the noise lifts around her
she remembers the silence
she feels something tug at her
she ignores whatever it is

The Boy Through the Sea

she writes of a boy
and the sea
she doesn't tell me his name
just that he was there
diving through rain
for oysters

on Sundays, she said
he worked with apples
his hands hardened
like pointed fences
watching him mold
the fruit
she captured his smile

small things, that is all,
the sea, instead of love
instead of the boy
watching the sound of the waves
against her feet
she sees him there beside her
she holds the sea in her arms

Watching Jacarandas

Afterward, she stays away from talking,
writes of small things
Kentucky fresh dew on jacarandas
leaves curving into soil
she spent two hours feeding, cultivating
watching the tree

she spends her time planting
trying to make something work
getting love from nothing
she sees the sun stain the trees
watching, she feels something
small beginning

New York Fields

with every breath
she dies inside
he does not know
she doesn't love him
he knows
only the outside
her hair falling down
in New York fields
his hands between its ripples
being beautiful to him
was enough
their hands engage
instead of their minds
they walk through streets
listen to faraway music
in the city
with its flowers
she lies between teeth
dreaming of someone nameless
with his whisper
she falls silent
until everything goes limp around her
across telephone wires
he says love carefully
smiling at the thought
she reveals nothing

The New Year

the curve of your arms
told those men
their mother was here
you could be anything
anyone wished for

after all this time
your face cracked, falling off
you reach
you say you will have a house
in New York

a second husband, children
a New Year's Eve Party
with champagne
in those fluted glasses
a sequined dress

you can see it all now
in the mirror above your bed
the man reflected
perhaps he
will fall in love with you

Orchid Islands

The first time I saw them
you were standing by my window
orchids in your hand

in time they were placed on the counter
you gave me a rose to place in the middle
a stranded mass of purple
with that one white rose

the scent filled the room
my eyes, ears, were everywhere
growing larger, filling everything
an island of orchids calling us

in time I was set aside
priorities calling you
I stood in the middle of the house, rigid
your gifts around me like water rising

I began to rest my life on these flowers
lifting them around my head like a life raft
touching those orchids, their colors
bled on my fingers, staining them purple

their scent in my hair, on my neck,
dizzying me, you watch me floating
you see my eyes are no longer open
you smile

Softly to Her Children

she came with good intentions
she had saved her husband from his guilty family
carried him across the country
to a life complete with the trimmings
she had given up being something separate

she says to me
someday you will know what I have done
look where I came from
she points to her relatives
strung out on bitterness
lives that cast no shadows

she raised everyone high above her
the years where she didn't know
what she wanted
what is left now
in the perfect home with the perfect husband

she remembers singing
softly to her children
she sits now with her husband
the children have left
she has learned how to sew

she embroiders a scarf for her children
it tells a long story
she sews by candlelight
as her own mother sewed
until she is felled by sleep

Canyon Dust

She left for the Grand Canyon early
while dust settled in a film
over his windows

He followed
although
he had known

from the moment
he created her
conjured up some vision

of her hair
He knew she would leave
he told himself

hands on steering wheel
to him She meant nothing
Her image was enough

to sustain him
She had been so close
to his perfect woman

He took out a photograph
The world closed around him
He stood partway down the Canyon.

A bird flew up into rain
In the beginning she was vulnerable
but not quite empty enough

The perfect empty shell
of a woman
that was what he wanted

He sees her high above him
clenching her hands
not seeing him

He cannot decide whether to call to her
She rocks back and forth
like a pendulum

He clenches a stone
heavy weighted unmoving
He wants to walk away start over

Above him he hears the woman
singing in a language
he does not understand.

Selecting Houses

She says
she would like a house
in the country
away from cars freeways
He wants an adequate building
with controlled garages
suitable parking
At my house I see her
she says five minutes ago
I stopped crying
he thinks I am beautiful
that I am enough
so it does not matter
Out my window
we watch children play through grass
what can we say
ah the children they love him
yes she says and smiles
as if sustained
he says we will compromise
on our house
she wants to laugh
we begin to write
I see her two days later
brown hair shows through blond
her skin begins to peel off
he has found it she says
not hearing herself speak
she draws flowers on paper
it is small brown
large steps running up to the door
his work is five minutes away
it is good, she adds
she reaches into her purse
for the picture of it

look she tells me
the bars on the window
are shining
I see her behind them
the children in her lap
waiting for him
to come home
I hand it back to her
she creases it
returns it to her purse
she laughs a practiced laugh

Praying Lilies

the girl kneels as ritual
on the floor gathering lilies
in her arms
her skin dark
her black hair coarse
braided to uncover her face

her feet turned inward
almost touching
each other's toes
they curve
in the center
like stems of flowers

her skirt creases
at mid-calf
her exposed skin trembles
she waits for her father
the floor presses against her knees
she cradles the lilies

she would like
to become them
she prays silently
to be taken away
the lilies curve toward her
until they surround her

the floor becomes harder
flowers scrape her back
she bleeds onto them
stems pull her hair
she weeps silently wiping her face
until it pools in her hands

she falls to the ground
hears prayers rising around her
for her father's demise
the lilies are speaking
or the blood on her fingers
she touches her lips in silence

December Cold

She built the house
so in an earthquake
it would fall
in fires go up in ash
in floods wash the trees
like driftwood

Her parents' house collapsed
after years of Father tinkering
Mother crying into her tea
they talked with separate lawyers
agreed it was a total loss

It was all she expected and more
the cold the fragile house
the never knowing
whether he liked her
or just being in a house
and there she was

The sun rises through
window cracks
the dust magic
everything perfect
in the light of December

Perhaps pity could make her beautiful
catching sympathy
in smiles and touches from him
they could talk about parents
they could talk at a table through
the metallic clatter of silver

If she would die
he would wrap himself
in everything she touched
that would be all right
there would be nothing

he says they should walk
gets her heavy coat
she smiles at how he loves her
a deep sympathetic love
that would never go away
never go away she thinks

Until death?
ah she laughs
becoming intrepid
with the wind in her face
they continue to walk

Maybe I could fall she thinks
I know he would pick me up
he clasps her hands encircles her wrists
her eyes flare for a hopeless second
then resigned
that is the end of her wishes

Where would you like to walk
he asks, she shrugs
anywhere
secretly she wants somewhere cold
where the rain is in her hair
she is numb like death

In That Room Without Breathing

she sits
in that room
waiting for news of her son

doctors are everywhere
she cannot sit
without the walls caving in

crushing her
her blood pooling on the floor
she can't remember what

she was doing yesterday
her hands clasp
her skirt

she looks to her husband
what? is something
the matter?

she cannot feel without thinking
she begins to get warm
a sticky clinging feeling

what can she say
she wishes she could hold his hand
her husband's

smoke moves up the wood panels
like snakes into the roof
she watches as habit

she can't hear now
she can't see the smoke
she can feel it climb the building

she is careful not to speak
out loud
not to breathe
the smoke melts in air

she remembers
when he was young

his baby hands in hers
she does not know what happened
a sound is heard outside

those shoes are walking toward her
okay she says
breathing faster

the shoes remain faceless
they walk past her and it is alright
her husband

is smoking again
ah she wants to
throw herself

against the walls
scream with her hands clenched
her legs crossed

her sweater buttoned tightly
the rings in place
she is trying to imagine

where the smoke is
in the air in his body
lining the clouds

she tries to hold on
she wants to fly
into the framework

float on that cloud of smoke
be nothing
but his mother

everything dies around her
the walks her husband her body
what what else?

she thinks
she sees the smoke circle envelop her
sometimes that disappears too

On a Couch With Pasta

I think I was with you last night
your arms around me pressed the window
as you left

you taught me to love
now work calls you
I am part of the house

I try to remember life before you
but the window is too clouded
for me to see out

last night I threw myself down
failed to get dinner
the house did not care

I made dinner with you home from your last trip
I watched your eyes but they stayed with me
until wine and sleep took you

my hands through pasta cooked and warm
I sit on the couch
twist my hair like noodles

it is hard to see through the curtains
they stick shut I can no longer see out
I am the legs of the chair

while you are gone I mold my thoughts like bread
when you return
I will not have moved

Rice and Loneliness

when he thinks of her
he cannot help
but remember
her hands

in her hair
shaping his body like sculpting
the way they felt
to touch

he knew
when he came home
she would be there
waiting for him

not a hollow
piece of art crafted
out of a woman's
skin hair

but his
answer to fear
loneliness her voice
arms that carried him

he thinks
of yesterday
wasn't her lotion on the table?
her brush filled with her hair?

that hair
he would take and hold
and watch fall to her back
covering her body

she was gone
long before her memory
caught up with him
and he had a chance to hold her

he hasn't left her room
he holds her scent around him
he thinks, maybe
I will keep her clothes

with the car keys in his hand
he cannot bring himself
to find the grave, he is afraid
of getting lost, never finding his way home

the children are not home
they will not know, he says
as if he is a criminal
in his car, hands on the wheel

he stares at the lines
drives through
woods, following
parted fields

finally, beside
what is left of her
he stares at the sky
sits down

near a tree
the grass has turned brown
he grows old
watching her dance

he remembers her face laughing
rice thrown toward her
her cooking brown rice
white rice Spanish rice

her hair fanning
around her body
until
she is on the ground

he lives in the direction
of the setting sun
it is time to drive
the children will need rice

their favorite
he will cook it
he will feel her hands
running through it

like she ran her fingers
through his life

Light Underneath Glass

You don't hear me.
All our days together
collect.
I melt in them,
return to that position
outside a window.
The sun is hot.
My hair is red.
I am in prison.
I came to you,
turned you to that sheet
of what was done to you.
That day in your arms.
I left, fading,
my hands shaking.
Always I am on my knees
crawling
underneath glass.
The light turns on, off
like the changing of us,
the beginning
of our new routine.
I wait,
press my hand against
that window.
If only I knew I wanted you.
I miss your reflection
in the sun.
You are underneath yourself,
your ears cover
my lips.
I tell you what you know
turn myself on, off
light beneath glass
darkening.

Her Uncovered Face

She feels the sun
against her house
she is inside
the covers over her face
thinking nothing
she counts the days
seconds before he enters
she clasps her hands
the phone rings
she thinks
if it were him
I would know
I would feel it
pick the phone up
that's it
it cannot be him
besides what would he want
with me
he said
wait for me
she is in bed
with her clothes on
drowning from waiting
she becomes old
in weeks

he walks in the door
uncovers her face
she doesn't want him anymore
stay
he says
you said you would wait for me
she opens her hands
fingernails chewed
she passed the point of wanting
days ago
go
he leaves again
it has been months
no one to uncover her face
to make her wait
to make her breathe

Dancers in Her Hands

"For all of us, but especially for a dancer...
there is a blood memory
that can speak for us."

"People ask me why I chose to be a dancer. I did not choose. I was chosen to be a dancer and with that, you live all your life." Martha Graham

She speaks of dancers,
her life of ninety-six years,
the blood memory that carries
through dance.

People remember her
hands over her eyes
in a chair, creating,
rocking like a pendulum.

Martha, sitting in her studio,
quiet, the energy reshaped
from her dancers, her hands
feel the air.

I see her on stage
holding the hands of dancers,
smiling, the audience does not
see her cracked face, wrinkled skin.

They listen to the sound
of her body speaking,
the blood from generations
flowing through her hands
outstretched, her feet lifting her
across the stage into the light,

the dance becoming a creature
alive, twisting, made up of dancers
forming stories that we see every time
for the first time.

Nothing and Everything

the dancer sits next to the old woman
her legs molded
from plies, pointe shoes
clair de lune floats off mirrors

the old woman
wears black
an extended mourning
her stockings protect her skin

she was seen pirouetting at the Met
her ears remember music
French instructors telling her
what wasn't enough

her life crafted
around money and men
one telling her body to do this
the other that

her purse hugs her fingers
which arched across the barre
cupped men's faces
they flew away into photo albums and urns

sitting on the
cracked wood bench
her leotard reveals
nothing and everything

between love and dancing
she doesn't know
which to abandon first
one is the excuse for the other

a young dancer takes her shoes off
their molded exterior
falls weightlessly
into her bag

standing up
she wonders
if he is outside
waiting for her

picking up her bag
she sees the older woman's feet
pointed outward
feet that remember dancing.

For a Quiet Sun

Lover, go fast now.
That golden hat is waiting.

Your hair in my hands
the sun to our backs.
Take my hand
kiss my fingertips, remember?

See the clouds rushing our loves
like quiet peregrins flying off.

The way she walked, how the sun
hit the left side of her white face.
Oh you, running against the sand
with your paper, your feather pen.

Do you see? how easily
ink slides, like words dropping off?

Look for me, blinded by the sun.
I am that shape you can't see.
Her hat holds her together
I am the water flowing past you

You are a branch reaching into me
I have left you this quiet sun.